For Stephanie
this journey
into the dark night
of the soul
I claim you. Yes!

Love,
Dave
June 2005
Coos Bay

Driving and Drinking

Driving and Drinking

a poem by David Lee

drawings by Dana Wylder

Copper Canyon Press : Port Townsend

Cover art: *Old Red Truck,* by John Carlander

Special thanks to Fred, Willa, and Glen Miller for that August evening, to Ron Roper for and about trappers, and to Willa Mina Gerber for and about perpetual motion and bathtub gin.

Copper Canyon Press is in residence under the auspices of the Centrum Foundation at Fort Worden State Park in Port Townsend, Washington. Centrum sponsors artist residencies, education workshops for Washington State students and teachers, Blues, Jazz, and Fiddle Tunes festivals, classical music performances, and the Port Townsend Writers' Conference.

LIBRARY OF CONGRESS CATALOGING-IN-PUBLICATION DATA

Lee, David, 1944 Aug. 13–
Driving and drinking : a poem / by David Lee ;
   drawings by Dana Wylder.
      p. cm.
   ISBN 1-55659-208-6 (pbk.)
   1. West (U.S.)—Poetry. I. Title.
   PS3562.E338D7 2004
   811'.54—dc22

                                    2004045536
SECOND EDITION
98765432
FIRST PRINTING

COPPER CANYON PRESS

Post Office Box 271
Port Townsend, Washington 98368
www.coppercanyonpress.org

for John and Laverne Sims

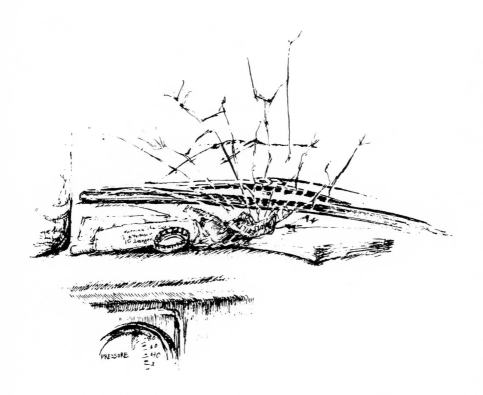

North to Parowan Gap

Turn right up there
and get off these pavements
there aint no sense
to holding up the traffic
and we aint hurrying
you just turn there and that dirt road
goes out to the Gap
where them Indins wrote on them rocks

I remember the first time
I ever got drunk. Me and my brother
we was following this branch back home in Misippi
when we seen a trail leading off

and he knew but I didn't
he's oldern I was and been down them trails
so's we went down and found it
any time you find a trail off a branch
you follow it it'll take you to a
still that's how them revenuers find them
or maybe somebody's shithouse
but that'll be by their house close
so you know so's anyway
we found it and they had all this beer
that's the first boilings out of the mash
before they make the whiskey
and my brother he broke off these cane stems
to make straws and we got to sipping
that beer by god I passed out
I hadn't had that befores and he got scairt
and had a hell of a time getting me home
where he told Mama he didn't know what happened
maybe I fell or got snake bit or cow kicked
cause she'd of beat him into next week
if he sed I was drunk cause I was too little
Mama about had a worm of course
I don't remember I was passed out
and thot I wouldn't live cause her brother
got kicked in the head and woke up a idiot and
stayed that way naturally he got kicked
by a horse you can still see the print of that horseshoe
on the back of his head
he don't look a day older than the day it happened
so she went for the doctor
that was quite a trip we lived
12 mile outside town and didn't have no car

she walked the whole way but the doctor he give her
a ride back that doctor he come
looked at me and he sez he'll be okay
soon as he sobers up and they say Mama cried
and raised all kind of hell
the next day was my birthday and I was 9
I guess that's why I member
she was so mad she made me a cake
after I eat a piece she thowed
the rest away and wouldn't let nobody else have none

so's this other time we found this branch
and went down there was the biggest still
I ever seen they was making barrels of whiskey
by the wagonload and I don't know how
they did it that still wasn't 2 mile from our house
we never seen no smoke nor smelled it
we figgered maybe they's shining at night
it must of been white folks or rich niggers
(that's what we called them back then) cause
they had money so me and my brother
we went home and hitched the wagon to come back
we stoled 2400 pound of sugar
in daylight, Lord Jesus that was stupid
we could of been shot but I guess nobody seen us
I heard God takes care of kids and idiots
that's where my brother he got his finger cut off
we was hurrying and he must of got
his finger in the leaf springs and I thowed
this sugar up and he sez ouch and that's all
till we's almost home and he sez look here
I done cut my finger off and it was gone for sure

11

Driving and Drinking

Mama got scairt but we hid it and
give most of it away or fed it to the hogs
we didn't have no money so that was a good find
me and my brother we went back the next day
when Mama wasn't looking cause she sed
to keep our butts out of there or we'd wake up dead
them shiners they don't want no companies
but they wasn't nothing there
they'd moved that whole still that night
so's you couldn't tell it'd ever been there
we looked around but didn't find
his finger it was gone too and
we never heard a sount

Mama she made wine at home
outa berries and grapes and stuff and we'd hep
she'd make little jars for us
but wouldn't put in no sugar so it wouldn't
make no alcohol just grape juice
when she'd get to working we'd get that sugar and
slip it in the jars and close them up while she didn't know
she thot it was fine we was drinking juice good
for vitamins in the wintertime
we thot it was fine too

Mama just whupped me bad one time
because I was the youngest
it wasn't my fault I didn't mean no harm
I found this bull snake and put him in the corn crib
to eat up the mice that was eating the corn
leaving rat shit all over to stink
them rat turds make a building smell up

worse than skunk piss cause it don't go away
stinks like sorry folks live there
so I thot it'd be a good idear
but I forgot about it until Mama
she went out to get some corn and grabbed holt of
that snake because she couldn't see good
in the dark and I was standing there in the door
heard her yell by god she come out of that crib fast
and couldn't let go of that snake
she choked it to death and beat me with it
all the way back to the house
I'd of rather she'd of used a switch
by then I was scared of that snake too
it hurt like hell I won't pick up no snake
now for nobody. But it did eat up
a whole buncha mice so it wasn't a real bad
idear like some I've saw

this other time we
lost our milk cow and had to go find her
we let her run loose but this time she didn't come back
so we went to look and we found this still
these niggers was running. It was niggers we knew
so we started talking but they wouldn't give us
no whiskey because they knew Mama would kill them
if she found out and she always did
we just talked for awhile about whiskey and wimmin and
Jesus things niggers talk about and after a time
here comes Mama and we thot we'd bought the farm
cause we posta be looking for the cow
and had forgot about that
Mama she didn't say nothing but just walked up

stood there awhile and then she sez
what you niggers got buriet over there?
and we seen this grave we hadn't noticed before
but we could tell it was a grave
aint it funny how you caint never get a grave
hid to where it don't show?
them nigger men went to stirring
one sed oh no miz Sims that aint no grave
she sed don't you lie to me Leonas Johnston
that's a grave and you done kilt my milkcow
and buriet it there Leonas he sez
no ma'am we aint done kilt yo milkcow
that aint what's buried theah she sez to me
and my brother to go home and get the shovel
so we'll just see cause it was a fresh grave
them niggers all come over then they sez
now miz Sims we aint seen yo milkcow
she sez for them to all go strait to hell they done
kilt it and buried it them niggers got to dickering
they give Mama a hundred dollars for our cow
so we wouldn't dig it up the cow wasn't
worth that but she took the money and we went home
2 days later that cow come back with a new calf
we didn't know she was gonna have Mama
sez now aint that something? I lived there
12 more years and I never did go back to see what
was in that grave I really didn't much
want to find out I guess

that dam cow got us in all sorts of troubles
she's always running off and we couldn't find her but
we never done too awful much shining ourselves

just wine and a little whiskey for us now and then
Mama she never liked it much
but this one time it got rough we didn't have
no money at all and the crops didn't come in
sides the revenuers had put the hammer down
and the reglar shiners cut off
so me and my brother we thot wot the hell
we needed money and besides if they caught us
they had to feed us in jail baloney and grits and gravey
we set up this little still not much
but we made this deal for 30 gallon in pint jars
and that'd help a little to get thu winter
we cooked her up and it was a good batch we
made us some too and got it all put up in the cellar
on Saturday night these niggers was gonna come get it
but me and my brother we got this other job killing hogs
so we had to go that day but sed we'd be back fore night
well that morning here comes this law
he knocks on the door but Mama seen him coming
she hid and wouldn't open the door he yelled
and knocked for a long time and looked all over
in the yard and shithouse and barn but he never
opened the cellar and then left
Mama she's scairt she carried all that whiskey
out to the barn and poured it out on the ground
and warshed the jars and then busted up the still and
buried it so by the time we got back it was done
and that evening here come the law again
he knocks on the door and Mama sez what you want?
and he sez Miz Sims you know whar your cow is?
she sez my cow? he sez yas
she sez what cow? and he sez you only got one cow

she sez oh that one? he sez yas and it's breechy
and done broke down 3 fences and knocked down
a shithouse and kicked a dog and mebbe broke its head
open but she found her a bull by god and she's bred
and you gotta come get her right now
she sez oh that one and he sez yas so my brother
he went with him to get her and then Mama
she started bawling she sez oh John I thot he's after
the whiskey and I sez no just the cow the whiskey's okay
she sez oh no it aint and I sez what?
so she took me to the barn to show me where she
poured it out by god there was 3 sows and all their pigs
laying there deader'n hell I sez what the shit?
Mama sez oh my god I done kilt our hogs
I sez I sez what the hell's going on? she sez
the law's here before and I thot he's after the shine
so I poured it all out and it kilt our hogs
and she commenced to bawling real bad and I felt sorry
but when I looked again them hogs wasn't dead
but they's so drunk they couldn't get up
and could only barely breathe
it was 4 days before we could get them out
of that barn and then they'd break back in
ever chance they'd find and it was all that cow's fault
but them niggers never did even come to buy it anyway
I never did find out why not
but we didn't make no more whiskey to sell
Mama sez she couldn't take that no more

I always had the bad luck
finding dead bodies
some people have the touch for it

some just don't. The first one
besides what might of been in them nigger's grave
was this feller that they thot was lost
and put him on the radio for everbody
to look for so we all went out to hep
I found him but he wasn't lost
but dead he was in his car by this dirt tank
where he'd drove to shoot hisself
he couldn't shoot straight for shit
he'd meant to put the pistol in his mouth
and blow his brains out the back but he missed and
shot his face off but he was dead
I always wondered if it hurt or not
the dumb sonofabitch
they couldn't even open his box at the funeral
so's we could see most people
just had to take my word for it

and then this feller got drownt in the river
we had to get him out because the fish
would eat him then you couldn't sell no fish
to the niggers for a month they'd think
they's eating people or something
we'd get out the boats and the hooks
and drag the mud
sometimes you'd find him sometimes not
we'd always spread the word we'd
got him out and they wasn't no fishbites
this time we couldn't raise this one so
we all anchored up in the river
and they blowed up dynamites in the water
to make him float up

Driving and Drinking

I don't know why that works but it does
I had this nigger friend in my boat
he was drinking whiskey and they
blowed some up by us blubblubblub
here he come up right beside us
by god it like to of scairt me to death
he floated right over to my boat
so I hooked him when I looked at that nigger
he was all white like me he was scairt so
I sez do you reckon we oughta pull him
in the boat with us? he sez whar?
and I sez in here and he sez whar
in this boat? and I sez yas and he sez mista John
if you let him in this heah boat I's getting out
right now I sez Heavy you caint swim
and he sez whar? so I sez heah
just like the way niggers talk
he sez mista John if they's to let some nasty dead man
in the boat with Jesus he just gets out and walks
on the watah what's good for Jesus is good fo
Heavy that's whar I sez to myself that's good for me too
I don't like touching no dead body neither
and won't do it that's what they pay them
people who go to college to learn how to do it for
but I acted like I was going to pull him in
Heavy he dam near turned that boat over
he was getting out I mean right now
by the time they come got him from us
and we got back to shore Heavy he was so drunk
he couldn't walk to his car I heard he
went and got babtized again next Sunday
he's so scairt

18

this other time I was running my trot line at night
I didn't have no license
and I was pulling my line in when it stuck
so I thought it was snagt or I had me a big catfish
on so's I took a wrap on my hand and
pulled hard it moved a little not much
so I wrapped it rount my back
like you hold a big hog with a nose loop
give a big pull and felt it give so's I pull
hard and hold my lantern out there's
somebody's arm sticking up out of the water
broke off his body at the shoulder
right in front of me oh my lord
it scairt me terrible I peed right in my boot
I got out of there
finding bodies in the daytime's one thing
I aint staying around them at night
I called the sheriff and told him
he went and got it I heard
it was some feller who'd got wrapped up
in a chain and he fell in the river
I don't know how he done that
they was a reward and he kept it the sonofabitch
I couldn't do nothing
I didn't have no license
to run that trot line
by god sometimes I just hate the laws

I run a fish boat for years
on the river it was a good way to make
a little money back then
during the depression it got so bad

to where one time the auction only offered us
a dollar apiece for top hogs then charged
20 cents to handle so's we had to take
over a hundred head out and shoot them
cause it wasn't worth it but I could
make enough to get by poaching fish
and selling them to the niggers
turtles too I never knew what they did
with them turtles but for awhile I'd go out
with a dip net I get a warsh tub full
of baby turtles so's this man he'd come
give me a dollar a hundred
but the law come and made me quit
else he'd make it hot so's I couldn't sell fish
no more I've always wondered if he was
selling turtles too
I'd buy 5 gallons of whiskey and then fill
these half pint jars half full then put water
soaked in tobacco in the rest and take
the whiskey and the fish to town
I'd pull up and honk here'd come
these niggers I'd sell them a half pint of whiskey
and a fish for a dollar but not just whiskey
I aint never been a bootlegger
they had to buy a fish or they couldn't have no whiskey
I'd wrap up the fish in newspaper
which was good cep I'd draw a crowd
round my car I'd have to keep moving round town
so's the law wouldn't start wondering
and come see they didn't much like selling whiskey
to niggers fish was all right
but fish never drew no crowd

them niggers would give me the nastiest dam dollar bills
I ever saw here'd come a big old fat woman
she'd reach down between her boosums
and pull out this piece of paper that you couldn't
even tell was money it was so greasy
I was almost ashamed to spend it
but not quite so I'd sell for awhile
then drive down a ways and honk and
sell some more one time I drove 5 miles
to the next town and was selling and here come
this nigger who'd walked the 5 miles to buy more whiskey
he still had his fish wrapped up in newspaper
under his arm Christ almighty I sold a lots of fish
that way. But then one day I got caught
the law thowed me in jail so I left Misippi
fore my trial I aint lived there since
that sheriff he's still the law and that's been 25 years ago
so's I just go back to visit sometimes.

Pull off up there at the Gap will you
this here beer's hanging between my kitneys
and knees I better let some out.
We'll get on another road up there
we got plenty of time we can
put the lights on the rocks and
look at them Indin pitchers for a minute
we aint in no hurry are we?

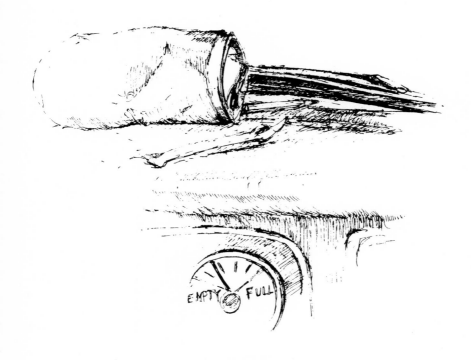

East to Paragonah

We can go down this road now
it'll take us to Paragonah
but then you know that being as you
live there it's still a good place
and we got plenty of time.
I mean when I was a kid
we had to make our fun
there wasn't no movie houses nor
money to raise hogs
and if you did have it they sold
for a dollar less than
nothing. We had to get by
with what we could find.

Driving and Drinking

After I left Misippi
I and this friend was building shithouses
during the depression and
we stayed in the upstairs of this gas station
in Kansas where we'd already built
these crappers out back
so when it got bored in the evenings
we went out to the women's
and drilt a hole beneath the seat and
built in a whupper made like a ping pong paddle
on a wire so when we pulled
it'd flap up and whop whop whoever was
sitting on the throne on the ass
but she couldn't see who was whupping

the first was this lady tourist
in a out of state car without a husband
who didn't buy no gas but
just ran out back and we didn't know
if it'd work right so we waited
till we knew she'd be all hunkered good
and pulled hard twice and heard it
whop whop on her fat butt
Great Christ Jesus Almitey she yells
and comes running out of that shitter
her drawers down around her ankles
they didn't have no lasticks
back then the govament kept all the rubbers
to hisself but her drawers was stretched
out a yard at the top around her feet
when she run back to her car
we thot that was pretty funny

but she didn't buy no gas

about the same time
we had what we called the Great Shit Race
this guy Henry who was my friend
was real big he must of weight 250 or so
when somebody new would stop in town
who was little Henry'd start going on
about how he could beat me in a foot race
carrying a man and me not and
he'd bet money on it and pretty soon
this little guy would hear the money
and he'd sidle Henry and offer to be
carried for halves and Henry'd okay
and we go to race
outside town Henry'd lay down
on the ground on his face and he'd have
the little guy lay on him upside
down and tie him to Henry's back tight
with a rope cause Henry sez
it's easier to run that way
and when he stood up the guy's feet's
sticking up in the air because he's tied on
upside down and we line up and say go
and Henry runs a little ways and then sez oh
OH I gotta go to the bathroom and drops
his pants and squats
and that little guy's looking at him square
eyeball to asshole and he starts yelling oh no
please don't shit on ME and we all
have a laugh
we done this a few times till onct

this guy was tied on Henry and when he
squats down that little fucker sez
you big sonofabitch you shit on me
I'll bite your nuts off real loud
and that scared Henry
he wouldn't Great Shit Race no more

there was this other lady
she came to the station in a big black car
and had a nigger driver who waited
and watched while the car got filt
while she went to pee so we snuck around
behind and pulled on the wire so
her ass'd get slapped and she by god
broke the door off she came out of there
so fast never yelled or nothing
but she was still holding her dress up
around her waist so's she wouldn't pee on it
and couldn't stop she was running
as fast as she could pissing 10 feet
ahead of her I never knew a woman
could piss that far and got in her car
and the nigger drove right off and never
paid for the gas but Mel (who owned the
station) didn't mind because she
left her purse in the shithouse and
it had 50 dollars she never did
come back for

I made these fart machines
out of a piece of clothes hanger and rubber bands
and a warsher (this was after the depression

28

when I was more growed up) that I had
some fun with I'd go to the bar and put it
under me all wound up on the stool and then
at the right time I'd lean off and let it rip
on the plastic sounding like a big
butter bean fart and we'd get a laugh
one time I and Laverne went
to this bar in Boise and I told the bartender
and he sez yas go ahead and in comes
this Basque sheepherder that didn't have
3 fingers on one hand just a thumb and 1 other
to drink a beer and he sits down by me
the rest of the bar all but empty
but he's gotta sit right there so's I don't say
nothing for a while and then lean over
and let that warsher unwound
that Basque he don't say nothing he looks
at me and shakes his head and
I say I'm sorry I had these ham and beans
for breakfast my stomach's clabbored and he
pats me on the shoulder and nods and tells
the bartender to make me a alka seltzer
in my beer that'll feel better so while
he's not watching I wound the fart machine
up again tight and let it go again
real good
that Basque he grins and waves his hand
without no fingers and he sez
now is betta you don need no medichin
and Laverne whispers and sez you better stop now
but I wound it up again and then let it off
that Basque he looks at me hard

then he stands up and walks out to
the middle of the floor and he skips and lifts
his leg up high and he lets
the biggest fart I've ever heard and sez
HOW WAS DAT VUN?
and Laverne sez that's it I'm leaving
but before I can pick up my change he's
sitting back down and that fart
come with him all green
it was that kind that hangs on things
till it slides off and then lays on the floor
gasping and you know it's there and try not
to step on it because you can't get it
off your shoes and I sez
I didn't fart it was this machine
and he sez matchine?
and I sez yas and show it to him
and he sez vat do you guys
tink of nex time, huh?

the other one I member
was this old lady she came in a whole
carload and was crippled up to where
she had to walk with a cane
and I tell Henry we caint slap her ass
it'll break but he goes on down there
he was a crazy nigger
by god she must've been eighty
or more it took her a half hour
to get to the shithouse and she's in good
and we hear whop and wait to hear whop
again but before it can come

here she is out of that crapper
running like a racehorse
all her arthritices gone and her drawers
dangling on one foot all the way
back to the car and she gets in
and slams the door and the rest of them
we can hear asking her what happened
but she didn't say nothing
so's after they left I went down
to the shithouse and her walking cane
was still there and I've got it somewheres
if I need it and by god she
pissed all over that shithouse door
I guess I built shithouses for 3 or 4 years
all over that dam Kansas

well after that I got this job
as a lectrician with the lectric company
I went round stringing wire and
fixing wire that's how I first came here
I built wires through these mountains and sed then
I'd like to come back and figgered mebbe I would
aint it funny? I was a lectrician 2 years
and I caint make that dam pump
down in my well work goddam near busted my ass
getting down in that hole yesterday
and got spider bit and wet to my ass
it still don't pump I shouldn't never crawl down in holes

onct we was in Texas and there was this cave
with a long ditch running to it
that ditch sloped down to about 10 foot deep

with the cave at the bottom
I just had to go see what was in that hole
so's I walked down and went in and that's all
I member they was a deer in there
I didn't even know they was deers in Texas
that big sonofabitch come out of there
like a mayor out of a whorehouse
hit me right in the chest with his horns and
carried me out of that ditch and slung me off
at the top colder'n hell I don't even remember
being hit and it broke two ribs
they sed it was the biggest deer they'd ever saw
and I didn't even get to see it hurt so bad

then another time we was in Lousiana
we found this hole and I wanted to go in
so'd this nigger so I sez you go first and I'll foller
we crawled in all narrow as a chimley pipe
we could just barely get in then it opened up
in a room to where Wilber could stand up and he struct
a match and screams MAMA there's grunts
and we in a room full of them little javelina hogs
they's all scairt and trying to get out by god
somehow I got turned around in that tunnel
I still don't know how and come out something
else I don't know was how Wilber beat me outa
that hole but he did and still had the match in his hand
but it didn't stay lit I had hog tracks
all up my back them little fuckers just stomped
the piss outa both of us I never saw so many
in my whole life and don't want to again
I just don't know why God made holes in the ground for

one time I had to drive a long ways
to get to this other job I'd drove all day and half the night
I's tired and knew I couldn't drive no more
when I come to this one town I didn't know where I was
but there was this hotel so I stopped and went in
and rung the bell finally this man he come out I sez
I gotta have a room I'm sorry it's so late but I can't go
no more he sez well dam I'm sorry but we all full
I sez no shit? man I gotta find a bed somewheres
it's too cold to sleep in my car outside
it was winter and all
then he sez well there is this one room that has this
young feller in it he's a farm worker he sez
and come in for the weekend and there's 2 beds and
he sez if anybody needed the other one it was okay by him
so I sez that's okay by me how much?
he sez 4 dollars and that was fine so I paid him
and went up he was all asleep when I went in
so I didn't wake him up but just went to bed
a hour later I woke up but didn't roll over
just opened my eyes and he's standing there
without no clothes on but I could see he had
this big hard on sticking out all over
I looked around the room and couldn't see
no jar of salve or hand lotion or bar of soap or nothing
so I sez to myself by god he aint screwing me
he was just standing there still not moving
I laid quiet for a long time but I couldn't take it
I's afraid he'd holler and jump on me
or with that hard on just come and squirt
all over me and I wasn't gonna have that
so I finally set up and sez all right

Driving and Drinking

you just go lay down on your bed right now
he jumped like he never knew I was even awake
and I'd scairt him but he backed up and
laid down I sez pull them covers up over you
and he did so I got out of bed and sez
you move just one time and I'll knock your goddam
head off you hear? you don't move a bit
and he didn't he never even sed a word
I put my clothes on and went down and
rung that bell that feller he come out and I sez
I don't mean to be polite but you got queers
in that room and I aint sleeping with no queer tonight
I'm too tired and they aint even no vaseline
he sez oh my god I'm sorry I didn't know that
I sez that's okay I aint tired no more
so he give me my 4 dollars back and I drove
the rest of the night and got to the job
and worked all that day I's too nervous
but I've always wondered what I'd of done
if he'd stood there and squirted stuff on my bed
where he thought I's sleeping

we went to the deep south
that's where my stomach went bad
eating that soft homineys and drinking
skum water when we couldn't find fresh
I wouldn't feed no homineys to a hog I hate them
so bad I eat so many then
but we had a funny thing happen
it wasn't funny to them that got caught though
I's glad as hell it wasn't me
we was near this one town stringing this wire

34

and here was this nigger mayor or something
we'd find whole towns of nigger people
that wasn't on the map
we figgered mebbe they's slaves that scaped
fore the war and still didn't know better
wasn't no white people living there
he was fat and wore a black hat
and had a umbrella he walked under
like them Englishmens do
and had a big house in the middle of town and
a whole truckload full of women
we didn't know if they's wives or daughters
most of them young and pretty
so some of the guys on the crew got to slipping
down and taking the extrey ones out
in the bushes we all thought that was okay
he didn't seem to mind or notice
we was just passing through
anyway one day when we was about ready
to go on here he come with a bunch of his boys
they had chains and knives and guns
and he's walking under his umbrella
so he wouldn't get the heat stroke
we thot we's all dead
I was ready to sez to him I never screwt nobody
but nobody sed nothing
he walked around till he found 2 faces
he knew I heard later niggers sez we all look alike
to them if I'd known that then
they'd of had to shot me cause I'd of run
but he picked the right 2 and we just thot
they're dead what do we do now?

35

Driving and Drinking

but he had his boys
take their clothes off and then bend them
over a car hood and tie their legs up to the front
axle and their hands to the other wheel
so they's all stretched out tight
by then we figgered they'd castrate them
or cut them up and eat them or something
but we was wrong
we looked and seen 3 or 4 of the big ones
stripping off and then they greased up
their peters with white rose salve
by god they almost cornholed
them 2 poor men to death
and made us watch
I never seen something so horrible
them poor bastards was screaming for somebody
to shoot them and both bled out the ass
one of them I've heard is still crippled up
and shits all over hisself
cause his asshole don't work right
fucking around with the wrong people
just don't pay that's what we built
whorehouses and beer joints for

we went on and built the rest
of the line but by then I was getting sick
from all that shit I got inside me
it messed up my stomach real bad
to where I got to shitting and puking blood
they put me on the airplane in Alabama somewheres
and brought me home to have a looksee
I was in terrible shape they sed

36

mebic distribulatary or something
and put me in the hospital for a year and
cut all my guts out
they sed they took out 15 foot of guts
and most of my stomach
I was plumb eat up with that stuff
when I got out of the hospital
I only weight 96 pounds
they sed I probly wouldn't live
but I did though I wouldn't eat no homineys
or lye water grits for nothing
they had to give me all this blood
from other people
cause I couldn't hold mine in
and I kept getting sicker I got worried
I knew some of the blood was nigger blood
I didn't mind that
people who worry about that's stupider'n hell
it don't make no different
but they sez I got nemic
and I was afraid from that blood
mebbe I got that sick as hell nemic
that niggers get and die of
but they sed no it was different
I shouldn't worry about that
but I did anyways
I just couldn't help it

now I see up there
we already in Paragonah
I told you we'd get here
I think mebbe we better stop at your place

we're about out of beer
besides I'm about to pee all over myself
we got some time
I mean it's all
different now we didn't have
to get in all that trouble to have a little
fun back then we just made
our fun. Yep I miss them
times. I would of NEVER dreamed
a woman could piss that far.

Back to the Valley

I guess mebbe you better be getting me home
now, it's getting pretty late
and I'm getting pretty drunk
and tired
I got to get back on that swaker tomorrow
and cut hay, the bank
he don't give much of a dam
as to whether I'm having a good time
or not, he just wants his money on time
sometimes I think
if I gotta come back and wear out
another life like them Chinermens sez you do
mebbe I be the bank this time

Driving and Drinking

I know it'd be bout my turn
and mebbe his to let me hold the deeds
just onct
anyways that don't matter now
we got plenty of time
to worry bout that tomorrow
but I better get home and get some sleep tonight
so mebbe we better head on back

you know over yonder in them hills
Laverne's brother he found a Indin grave onct
it was a long time ago he wasn't very old yet
and he thot he'd just dig that grave up
to see if there's any jewlery or arraheads or other
Indin shit in there with that feller
so he come back to it one day
with a shovel and started digging
he wasn't very far along when he sez he felt
sorta nervous like he's about to pee
or something but he knew he didn't need to
he'd arredy had on the way
so's he went on and then got another feeling
like somebody's watching him dig so's he stops
and turns around and there's a Indin standing there
right behind him wearing them Indin clothes
like they don't wear no more
you know them leggings and that thing over
their chest and all and moskins
Laverne's brother he bout shit
cause he never heard nobody walk up
and he sez for a minute he couldn't say nothing
he just set there and finally he sez

what do you want? but that Indin
didn't say nothing just stood looking at him
and he sez I sez what do you want?
do you want me to leave? and when
he sed that that Indin just disappeared
right in front of him and never sed nothing
Laverne's brother he was scared
he got the hell out of there
and won't go back though he told me
about it and it happened up there
somewheres in them hills behind
that old mill I don't know for sure just where
I wouldn't go there for anything
I aint gonna fool around with that stuff

I heard about 2 men out hunting deer
in the hills that got lost
and it started snowing so's they had to
hunt around for a place to get in
and found this cave and when they went in
there's all this Indin stuff
jugs and arras and jewelry and stuff
and they had to spend the night in there and
they sez it's all haunted cause they heard
noises all night and couldn't sleep
so's when light come they filt their pockets
with all that shit they could carry and left
and finally found their ways home
but later they tried to come back and
get the rest of that stuff in the cave
cause it was worth money
but they looked all over and couldn't find it

again but they sez it's out there
and somebody'll find it one day
it aint gonna be me
I aint going in no haunted cave
for all the Indin jewelry in Chinar
it aint worth it to mess around
with no Indin ghosts
you just don't know what they might do

I aint talking about that no more
cause I get scared and then feel dam stupid
for doing it a growd man talking
about ghosts and stuff
oh I know they real I aint saying that
they just aint nothing I can do about them
and I aint for sure what they can do
about me so I just leave them alone
they was a haunted house back home
I was in and it made your hair stand up
on your neck when you walked in
didn't nobody have to tell you
you just knew something was wrong when you
walked in and you couldn't get a nigger
to go in that house for money
or whiskey and you couldn't thow
a cat through that house's door
it'd scream like hell and find someways
to keep from going in
cats and niggers they can tell things like that
that's why I won't have no dam cat around
they might just bring that stuff with them
I trapped a cat once or he got in my trap

I never planned it I wouldn't set no trap
for a cat and I was scairt to kill him
he might come back or bring something in
so's I just forgot about that trap for a month
and when I got back sure nough he's dead
but it wasn't my fault
I won't kill no cat but that's how haunted
that house was and I don't
much like thinking about it even now

here I caint get the top screwt off
this beer can you hep?
that's the onliest thing I miss this finger for
I got cut off I just haven't got no grip
to twist off these beer lids
they put them on too tight for me now

they was this guy I heard about
who was a miner or trapper or something
anyways he lived alone up in the hills
he got his finger chopped off
I guess mebbe he's a trapper and got it
caught that happens now and then
so he just picked up his finger and stuck it
in his pocket and went on home
when he got there he took out his needle and thread
and he sewed that finger back on
his hand but it didn't work
two three weeks later it all swoled up
green and the finger fell off
so's he built a fire in the stove
and then held the stump agin it

45

till he burnt all the green poison out
I think a feller'd have to be
pretty much of a man to do that

I knew this other guy who was loading up
a sow hog and she wouldn't go
so's he was trying to waller her into the truck
and he grabs her by the tail with
one hand and the ear with the other
she's screaming like hell the whole time
and him getting pretty pissed off
so's he does this a time or 2
and then he grabs her again but
gets the one hand in her mouth
he feels something pinch so
he pulls back his hand
and his finger's gone that dam sow's
bit him off he looked all round
and didn't find that finger nowhere
he guessed that sow swallered it

I don't much like to talk about how I lost
mine it still bothers me some
mebbe I'm just too drunk but I started thinking
about it. This all happened before
I went to work for the lectric company
I was younger and hired on for the oil
oh I made good money and it wasn't bad work
I don't think I'd do it again
anyways we's in Texas up on that panhandle
and had a rig drilling about 8 mile
outa town. We'd work 36 on and 12 off

at least I would cause I could make so much
I'd run chain awhile and then crownest
it never made no different
I was just after the paycheck on Fridays
I'd do bout anything they wanted as long
as the money kept coming in and they
seemed to like that
so anyways we was down over a mile
dam near 7 fousand foot
and we knew the oil was right there
we had to be coming thu any time
you just get the feeling it's gonna blow
so here comes the foman cause we sent for him
cause he has to sez when we can cap off
to get ready for the last push thu
so we don't blow all to hell and mebbe catch fire
that foman he's so goddam drunk
he caint tell shit from dog puke
he starts raising all kind of hell saying
you get this dam rig running right NOW
we won't hit no fucking oil
for 2 weeks nobody paid you to think
that's what I'm by god paid for
you just drill till I say stop and then
you just ast how long that's all
now git back to goddam work and stop
trying to set round fucking off
he left and we's so mad we couldn't see straight
for a man to talk to us that way
whether he's drunk or not didn't matter
so we set the bit back down in the night
and let her go wot the fuck

and about midnight the crewboss he sez to me
John you go up to the crownest we lifting
that pipe out I aint getting blowed up
for nobody and that was fine by me
we's all getting scairt to where we's just working
and not saying nothing just thinking
bout how long fore morning or till we got off
it's funny how you think the day'll take
the being scairt away but it never really does
anyways I climbt up the derrick to the top
and we's getting ready to pull that pipe out
when all of a sudden the whole thing starts shaking
to where I'm bout to get slung off
and I can hear the crewboss yelling
get down git DOWN this fucker's gonna blow
by god I burnt the palms off my hands
coming down I slid the wire guy rope
to the platform and then jumped off on the ground
the rest of the crew's arredy running ahead
so's I try to catch up and then I hear
that big sonofabitch touch off K-BOOM
right behint me and caught on fire
it blew me down on the ground and started
me burning by god I was scairt
I jumped up and started running and I'd of
burnt to death if this nigger hadn't grapt me
and thowed me down in this ditch and
put the fire out on my clothes
so's we look and that whole rig's burning
and we can see 2 guys from the crew laying
tween us and the rig burning up
and we know they's dead and

48

the rest of us is burnt bad where we might die
the crewboss he takes off running
into the fire and we can see he's gonna
try to bring the pickup out
he goes to it and grabs the doorhandle
and it's so hot part of his hand
sticks to the door and just comes off
but he gets in and somehows
he gets that dam truck started and drives out
of that fire I won't never know how
all the wires was burnt up
it got so hot that that truck's paint was all
scorcht off to where you couldn't tell even
what kind of a truck it was
and he brings it to us and we get in
I'm so burnt they had to put me in the back
and I'm laying in this feller's lap
who put out the fire in my clothes
and we pull out of there driving like hell
to get to town and by then the fire
was so hot it burnt up the whole goddam rig
there wasn't nothing left and I
seen it bend over just like it was plastic
I wanted to pass out so bad I couldn't stand it
but I didn't I just laid there and felt it all
and saw it all so's we're going to town
as fast as we can go and we pass this law
and he turns on his red light and chases us
till he gets close to see and then
he pulls ahead and leads us thu town
about 90 mile a hour to the hospital
where he jumps out and runs over and opens

the door and he just puked like hell
3 up front was arredy dead 2 of them
stuck together they's burnt so bad
and the crewboss's hand was off and he
didn't have no face left
how he drove God knows I don't
and there was only 1 other still alive and
he died that night so then they come
to get us out of the back and they started to lift me
out I sez get him first he saved my life
the man sez it's too late he's done dead
and I was laying in his lap

the onliest 2 that made it was me and
the crewboss. He was in the hospital for
96 days and I was in for 104
a week and a day more
I member cause he come to see me
when they let him out
he was burnt so bad I couldn't tell
who he was till he sed something
he ast if I's okay and I sed yas
we just looked at each other for a minute
and then he walked off
I sez be seeing you but he just waved
3 days later he drove his car
into a bridge and killed hisself
they buried him exactly 1 week after they
let him out and then let me out
the next day after his funeral was over

I don't have no bad scars left that show

my legs is burnt good
but I still feel it I get cold
and have to wear them long underwears
all year long on my legs
and my hands is so thin they bleed easy
my skin's bout as thick as a cigarette paper
and I don't have no feelings in my face
but I'm lucky I guess
all the rest is dead cept me

I went back to work for the oil
the next day because I didn't have nothing
else to do and they put me on chain
wrapping the pipes and that's when I done it
I hadn't been working a hour
when this feller on the other side
thew his chain and I felt it hurt
so's I finished and took off my glove
and the finger stayed in
I sez you sonofabitch you done
cut my finger off but I don't think
he heard he didn't say nothing
well I had it I went to
the man and sez that's it pay me off
oh he tried to get me to stay on
but I lost the taste
and didn't care no more

it was after that I went down south
and got my stomach cut out and
then I come here to die
it was a pretty place and I didn't have nothing better

Driving and Drinking

ever day Laverne'd pack me a lunch and
I'd draw her a map of where I'd be if I didn't
make it home I was weak and couldn't hardly
stand so I'd drive up in the hills
where I'd take off my clothes and let
the sun shine on me the muscles wouldn't heal up
on my stomach where I'd been burned
there was just ugly skin there you could see thu
I only weight 96 pounds and I'd lay
on a quilt and look back to the valley
and just wait to be dead and have it done

you know by god I guess I'd still
be laying up there waiting
cept after a while Laverne she went
and bought these 2 hogs for me
she knew I'd like that
I got to coming down early to feed them
and when I was up there   ·
I'd get to thinking about the market
and making money
I got so cited I come down one day early
and went to looking for a boar
to get a herd started
and the next day I forgot to go up to die
then pretty soon I bout quit
thinking bout it altogether
it just don't take much to keep
some people going

and that gets us bout to here
which is nearly home

time for one last beer
they say God takes special care
of children and idiots
I guess he's been watching out for me
by god I'll allus member them times
they was good times for the most
but I do hope to Christ they
don't never ever come back

Special thanks to Jim Swinerton
for his longtime support of Copper Canyon Press
and David Lee's poetry.